Colin E. Pyle was born in Salisbury, in 1968, and has lived in this area ever since. In 1980 he was hit by a lorry and nearly died, so passing his GCE 'O' Levels in English and Maths, RSA 1 Typing and 5 CSEs, was a reasonable achievement. He intended to work in the clerical sector but worked as a picker, in warehouses, for most of his life.

Colin joined various bands over the decades. Some of the creative moments, and performances, were very memorable and significant, while others were just a part of the journey to get to where he eventually arrived.

By the end of 2019, Colin finally released his first album and, by the end of 2022, Colin had released 11 albums and 4 singles as *The Lost Connection*. He now had a new job, new home, new live-in partner (his fiancée), over 1000 lyrics written, and around 250 songs recorded, which he had created, played and sung.

Colin now felt a sense of finality and closure after releasing '*Whatever Happened*'. He had been living in a dream for many decades and was now out of his bubble and finally living comfortably in the real world. The time was right to release this book.

I dedicate this book to 'You', Debbie Cofferon. Without her in my life I would never have been able to write the words that made this book so meaningful and complete. This is equally true about the effect she has had on my life.

Colin E. Pyle

THE WORDS BEHIND THE MUSIC VOLUME ONE: LOST IN REALITY

AUSTIN MACAULEY PUBLISHERS™
LONDON • CAMBRIDGE • NEW YORK • SHARJAH

Copyright © Colin E. Pyle 2024

The right of Colin E. Pyle to be identified as author of this work has been asserted by the author in accordance with sections 77 and 78 of the Copyright, Designs and Patents Act 1988.

All rights reserved. No part of this publication may be reproduced, stored in a retrieval system, or transmitted in any form or by any means, electronic, mechanical, photocopying, recording, or otherwise, without the prior permission of the publishers.

Any person who commits any unauthorised act in relation to this publication may be liable to criminal prosecution and civil claims for damages.

A CIP cataluge record for this title is available from the British Library.

ISBN 9781035828128 (Paperback)
ISBN 9781035828135 (ePub e-book)

www.austinmacauley.com

First Published 2024
Austin Macauley Publishers Ltd®
1 Canada Square
Canary Wharf
London
E15AA

Firstly, I must thank all of those that suggested releasing a poetry book. It was a good suggestion, and the advice was very much appreciated (even if some may have said 'Stop!' to my musical creations in the past).

A big thank you to Tim Kerley for creating the chords to 'We Won't Stop', as well as adding his guitar and vocals to the track.

Also, for providing the other necessities needed to make this book happen, I must thank Windows (for their Paint 3D app) and Microsoft (for Microsoft Word).

The poetic lyrics would never have come to life over the decades without my Yamaha keyboards (PSR-8000, PSR-9000 and PSR-9000 Pro); Mixcraft Workstation (Version 8 and 9); and DistroKid (for providing an excellent, inexpensive, online music distribution service through which I released my 11 albums and 4 singles). So, I thank all the above.

Finally, I must thank my fiancée Debbie, again, but not just for making my life complete and this book a reality, but for putting up with me constantly typing in every spare moment, to make this book publishable.

Table of Contents

Introduction	13
Album 1: Mask of Reality – Reality in Dreamland	14
What's the Meaning of Life?	16
Show Me a Road, The Right Road	17
Drink—Drunk—Blind	18
Love Music	19
Suzie	21
High	23
Make It Real	24
Give Me Time	25
Before (The Beginning)	26
Warning—Time for Change	27
Ten Years	28
Empty	29
Turn Down Suicide	30
Arrival… In Due Time	31
If Only (Pigs Could Fly at Christmas)	32
Just a Question (Before Things Get Heavy)	34
Engine With No Wheels	35
"Guarden Mind!"	36
Perseverance	38
Stick to Your Guns	39

It's a Deal	40

Album 2: Lost Property   **41**

Simple Man	43
Lost, But Never Forgot	44
Reflect	45
Never Too Old for This Stage	46
No Time to Waste	48
'All or Nothing' Kind of Man	49
'Write-On!' Track	50
Got What I Need	51
Connection	52
Solitary Writer	53
Never Too Late	54
The Lost Waltz Song Poem	55
Nobody Knows	57
This Is How It Is	58
New Tracks	59

Album 3: 2020 Vision   **61**

Life (We Live, Learn and Die)	63
It's My Medication	64
Drive	65
2020 Vision	66
One Big Army (Verses COVID-19)	67
Captain Tom	69
Love	70

While Furloughed	*71*
Two Shades of Blue	*73*
Between Dreams and Reality	*74*
Voluntary Redundancy	*75*
Freedom Seeker	*77*
'In the Middle' Kind of Man	*78*
Guilt Tripping on Happiness	*79*
A Maze in Life	*80*
In Time We Will Succeed	*81*
All Stars (Shine On!)	*83*
Key to Eternity	*84*
Time Will Tell	*85*
Album 4: The New Lost World 19-20-21	**87**
Rain on Me	*89*
Love in a Lower Key	*90*
Sunshine Mind	*91*
It's a New Day	*92*
Now I'm with You	*93*
Back to Work	*94*
Voices in My Head	*95*
I'm a Rebel	*96*
I Am Your Guiding Light	*97*
Winning Team	*98*
At the Top	*99*
Too Much	*100*

The 'Great' Rap Track	*101*
Mr Retro	*103*
Album 5: Whatever Happened	**104**
Won't Stop!	*105*
Shattering	*106*
(Feel the Vibe) With This Tribe	*107*
Ifs and Buts	*108*
I Am Just Me	*109*
The Fastest Man in the World	*111*
I Don't Like What I Do	*113*
The Best	*114*
Golden Anniversary	*115*
Beep! Beep!	*116*
Hot Dog	*117*
What Is Justice?	*119*
You	*120*
Forever Together, Me and You	*121*
We Won't Stop!	*123*
Epilogue	**124**

Introduction

Throughout the 1980s, I started to write down lyrical ideas while learning to play the keyboard. By the end of the decade, I finally declared my first lyrics complete. Since 1989, I have continued to write lyrics (and poems) and, as a keyboard player, have been able to turn many of them into songs.

In 1991-1993 I recorded songs with a young guitarist and vocalist, *Steve Emm*. When I was unable to find anyone else willing to sing my songs, I decided to try myself and, at the end of 1993, I had singing lessons.

It wasn't until I had released many albums, nearly 30 years later, that I decided releasing a poetry book based on m my album history, was a good idea.

Album 1: Mask of Reality – Reality in Dreamland

This is an album of songs that were used to create a story when I used to call myself 'Mask Of Reality'. Only a brief draft version was ever written. The story was created, and all the songs were recorded, between 1994 and 1998 (and the cover is a photo of the actual tape of the original recordings). The story has been amended since, but all the lyrics have remained the same (although an extra verse was added to 'Love Music'). 'Love Music' was updated in 2018 with LuZ on main vocals (a female session singer).

1. What's The Meaning Of Life?
2. Show Me A Road, The Right Road
3. Drink — Drunk — Blind
4. Love Music
5. Suzie
6. High

7. Make It Real
8. Give Me Time
9. Before (The Beginning)
10. Warning — Time For Change
11. Ten Years
12. Empty
13. Turn Down Suicide
14. Arrival… In Due Time
15. If Only (Pigs Could Fly At Christmas)
16. Just A Question (Before Things Get Heavy)
17. Engine With No Wheels
18. "Guarden Mind!"
19. Perseverance
20. Stick To Your Guns
21. It's A Deal

What's the Meaning of Life?

You say I look tired and don't get enough sleep
Drink too much and don't have enough to eat
I seem to be smoking more and more each day
But if I enjoy this life, isn't it right and whose to say?

I don't mind work, but it ain't really me
Leisure time's my pleasure — I live to be free
Some live to work, but I work to live
Times for enjoying and enjoyment's what I'm with.

I've got no lover, but why should I worry?
My interests I love — for a lover there's no hurry
I can't complain about one single thing
I drink to the future, reminisce on the past
And live this life for as long as it lasts.

I have no ambition — should I think about my future?
I want the easy life — to me it's much cuter
Now I'm getting older will I want a family
Or continue as I am, living leisurely?

What's the meaning of life?
Existence? Contention?
Progress? Happiness?
Success? Expansion?
Corruption?
Or love?

Show Me a Road, The Right Road

We're trapped within the prisons of our minds…
Which direction should we go?
The right road's hard to find.

We know the roads there are
But we don't know which to take
Just show me the way to go
What decision should I make?

We have to make decisions every day
Do we give it a go, or do we just stay?
We want to break free 'cos there's a whole world outside
We want to take the chances before the years pass us by.

Which way should I turn?
If I stay I'll end-up burning
Up in a ball of smoke
A wasted life without a hope
A wasted chance that passed me by
Should I stay, or should I try
To break away from this average life?
Show me the right road to take.

Drink — Drunk — Blind

Ignorance is bliss
When you're getting pissed
But ignorance is pain
The next day
I may not have been an alcoholic
But to be tea-total was a tonic
After a few heavy nights out on the town.

But then I look back on the good times I had
When living crazy on the town with the lads
All past memories are good I find
While bad times fall to the back of the mind.

Then a friend called me up one night
And asked me out for a drink I said, *"All right!*
He said, *"Time to reminisce with the old friends"*
With memories so many the night will never end
So I said, *"Yeh, sounds pretty good to me."*

At his local pub we all got together
The laughing and joking seemed to last forever
The conversation grew crazier, line after line
Before we knew it they were calling time.
Then a friend said:
"Let's continue drinking at your place or mine."

The rest is history, for which I can't recall
I woke the next day, sprawled out on the floor
My head was so heavy, I felt so sick
My stomach was a volcano, ready to spit.

We drink for the moment, while it lasts
Memories remain while the bad times pass
We live for the moment, we live for today
Ignorance is bliss — tomorrow's still a day away
Ignorance is pain!

This version of 'Love Music' featured on the album, was re-recorded at the beginning of 2018 and has changed its position in the story. This is a song that, in the context of the story, was performed in a nightclub by The Lost Connection (the older version of me) together with a female singer and inspired the younger me to write a similar song.

Love Music

I like to move
I like to groove, baby
I like to get down
on the floor.

I like to shake my body
I like to feel the heat
I like to move
To the sound of the beat.

Sing to me baby
Rock me to the floor
Show me that rhythm baby
Love me, love music, come on —
Love me more!

Let's shake it
Let's make it baby
Let's move
To the sound on the floor.

I want to rock all night
I want to rock and roll
I want to move
To the sound of your heart and soul.

We can shuffle, smooch and groove
On the floor it's time to prove
It's all about rhythm, all about feel
Let's get down and make it real.

All about love — how does it sound?
With this music it's time to get down
Make your move, do your thing
If you're in the mood let's hear you sing.

We're moving, we're grooving
We're shaking it while we're making it
I'm giving it while you're taking it
Together we're making it —
Love music!

'Suzie' was the song, in the story, that was written after being inspired by hearing 'Love Music'.

Suzie

I knew this girl called Suzie
But I wanted to know her more
Get to know her personality
Because she looked so stunning
And her smile I adored.

I saw her every day
Sitting in the library
Quietly reading her book
I didn't go to read
I just admired her looks.

Suzie — she moved me
No other girl did this to me
I watched her for hours on end
One day I was gonna have to
Bring my secret to an end.

I didn't need to talk or touch
Her looks excited me so much.

When I saw her, I fantasized
If only she realised
Only one way of proving this
I had to find the courage
To tell her how it is.

Throughout the week I learnt my lines
Waited for a convenient time
So one day, as she left
I finally got the chance
To get it off my chest:

"Suzie, you move me
No other girl's done this to me
I've watched you for hours on end
So I've come to ask you —
Will you be my girlfriend?"

It was all too much
We finally talked and touched.
She kissed me on the lips
And I shook at the hips.
My secret soon ended
As we intimately blended.

Suzie!
She's the one for me.

After discovering this newfound joy through music, it inspires this next song.

High

I don't need substances
I don't need smoke
All I need is a few notes
And I'm there:

High as a kite
My head in the sky
I'm gonna keep playing
I ain't gonna die
'Cos on this high
I can stay high and survive.

I don't need ten pints
And late nights on the tiles
I don't need drugs or money
Don't need any false smiles
I don't need short-while relief
'Cos I've got what I need
Music!

Way hey hey! You know I ain't low
I am happy wherever I go
And hey, I think you ought to know
Music's my drug — give me some notes.

With this music the higher I fly
With this music come and get high
With this music this is the life
'Cos on this musical high…
I can stay high and survive.

Make It Real

Some people it seems
Live their lives without a dream
Eat, sleep and go to work
At the end of the day what's it worth?

Okay, some say
When you've got no dreams
You've no chance of losing
Your destiny.

Negative — if you wanna live
Gotta have a dream.

Some people insist
You've gotta be a realist
You can't get a thing
If you've nothing to give
But who can say
What we've got inside
Just give it a shot
You've no reason to hide.

Take a dream, try to make it real
Try to do what you really feel
Take a dream, come out from within
Can't be a pessimist, gotta think positive
Take a look at how you live
And find what you've got to give.

Give Me Time

Give me more time, to get my mind together
And find where my priorities lie
There's so many things going on around me
But out of my desires no one has found me.

I live a life of work, with very little play
There just ain't enough hours in the day
The money I need, but I need time to breathe
And I just don't believe in this — the life I lead.

I walk feeling blind though knowing all my options
I sense there's a destiny, but I feel I'll forever quest
I want to take the chances, but my mind is disinclined
To change the life I'm leading, and I feel I'm going blind.

Give me time, give me space, to realise my place
To find the desire to establish my life
Give me time, give me more — what am I living for?
Freedom, money, love or success?
I'm gonna live my life doing what I find's best…
Just give me time.

Before (The Beginning)

I'm not striving for success
I'm just looking for happiness
For me, it's the only way
To enjoy my music which I love to play.

I'm not seeking wealth or fame
I'm getting by on the notes that I'm playing
I like what I'm doing
It will see me through
I like what I'm playing
I hope you do too.

Music — it's a soul provider
Music — it's my heart's desire
Music — an eternal fire
I couldn't ever live without music.

I get by doing my thing
Writing songs and learning to sing
Freeing my thoughts onto the page
This is the first stage — what is the next stage?
Waiting for the next page – what is the next page?
If I like what I've done, what will become?
Wait and see…
But either way, it's gotta be done.

*"In the beginning when things are simple
and they're done just for fun
The enjoyment's there, you haven't a care,
but then what becomes?
The better you get, you may regret
in a later time
When money gets the better of pleasure
and the fun then declines."*

I couldn't ever live without music.

Warning — Time for Change

Tick, tock, tick, tock
Hands travel around the clock
Things just remain the same…
It's time for change.

People are stuck in their ways
Living in their routine days
For them, there's no other way…
It's time for change.

Time for progression
Economising's the intention
Many things to be rearranged…
It's time for change.

Must save time, must make space
Cut down bills on running this place
Be constructive, remove obstructions
Initially, will cause disruption
But that's how it's to be

Better in the long run wait and see
Save money — increase production
Although maybe staff reductions.

Inevitable it seems
No other way
So understand when the bosses say…
"It's time for change!"

Voluntary redundancy was offered after nearly 10 years of working at the same place company, in the story.

Ten Years

I've nearly done ten years
The end of my sentence is nearly here
Working for this company, but soon to be
Looking for something else.

I've done my time, now I'm gonna break free
I'm gonna earn money, but how it suits me
Working for this company, but soon to be
Looking for something else.

My working life's been just wasted time
I'm gonna move on, now my job is on the line
Working for this company, but soon to be
Looking for something else.

Empty

When I woke, I went downstairs
Looked in the fridge and the cupboards all bare —
Empty!
Needed a cigarette, but none to be found
Turned on the radio and heard no sound —
Empty!

Looked for change but I couldn't find a penny
I need a job, but there just ain't any
Called for my friends but no-one home
So I went back all alone.

When you've got no job, you get so low
Life's so hard when you're on the dole
All my friends are still employed
My life can no longer be enjoyed.

I've got nothing left
I've got nothing but emptiness —
Empty!

Turn Down Suicide

I looked out the window, I wanted to go
But my body wouldn't let me — *Why?*
I just don't know
Life just seems to be getting me down
But I guess my body doesn't want to hit the ground.

"Turn down suicide
Make it through the bad times
Life is a playground
And one day the swings will swing your way."

I've had enough, I've got in too deep
I've got so many problems I can't get to sleep
At night I feel uneasy, nothing can please me
And the only way out for me is down…

Down below — out of the window
I want to go, but I haven't got the throw
I just need a blow, to help me out
To help me out of this strifeful life I'm in.

"Turn down suicide, even when the chance arises
Turn down suicide when it stares you in the face
When you feel your world's collapsing
and the walls are falling in
Don't let your urge to live
wear thin."

"It's such a shame when you're losing the game
You've got to keep going and hope things will change
Keep a little hope and rise above depression
The sun will shine brighter once the clouds have cleared."

"So turn down suicide!"

In the context of the story, 'Arrival... In Due Time' was a poem that was written on a piece of paper and found on the floor of the building in which 'Turn Down Suicide' was situated. It was recorded in 2019 as a spoken word track to make the album complete.

Arrival... In Due Time

People living lives contentedly
Within their set lifestyles
In an instinctive manner almost
Forgetting the mind is a free agent
Turning the wheels of industry —
The industry of life
From birth 'til death
All integrated like cogs
To form clockwork.

But time takes its toll
And lives will unwind
Eventually, time will freeze
Naturally
Stagnation would seem to be
The inevitable result
And many will stagnate
While others who possess the key
Will exploit the plenitude of time
And when the time is right...
Will call time.

The key to our destiny lies within
And eventually young budding minds
Will flourish and bloom
In the springtime and summer
Of their lives.

If Only (Pigs Could Fly at Christmas)

Christmas is a wonderful time
A time for celebration
When people give to the ones they love
Friends and relations
But the one that I
Am thinking of
Will never ever fall for my love.

I give her all that I can in the world
But she just thinks I'm crazy
Will she ever love me? I wish, oh I wish
That she could be my fish…
I'll keep living in dreams.

Presents are presented, and gifts to warm the heart
In the cold winter days when frost and snow may lay
But I feel lonely, sad and depressed
While people cuddle together in joy and happiness

And I keep seeing the same words:
'Happy Christmas', 'Happy Christmas'
Oh, how I wish…
If only!

As for the presents I sent her I hoped she liked
Okay, she thanked me, but just out of courtesy
Did she not wonder what had got into me?
Surely she could see how truly I loved her.

On Christmas Eve I heard a knock on my door
Was woken from my sleep in the middle of a dream
I opened the door, and I saw a blurred figure
That leapt towards me and gave me a big kiss.

She gave me a present, which she'd wrapped perfectly
And had taped to the top a Christmas card for me
She said I could open them, now if I wished
I agreed to do so but invited her in first.

And when I opened the card
I found the words:
'To my loving friend
With all my love and best wishes
From Miss… (kiss kiss kiss)'.

This was enough for me
The present I almost forgot
I stood in silence for a minute or two
But then heard her ask:
"Well, are you going to open your present now?"
On hearing this I peeled the paper
From the small slim box, to find a CD:
'Reality In Dreamland'
When I saw this, I quickly looked up
But only to see her vanish before my eyes—
If only pigs could fly!

Reindeers fly
Snowmen are alive
Father Christmas arrives
And I thought I saw a pig fly.

Just a Question (Before Things Get Heavy)

I love my music
I don't want to lose it
I don't want to use it
I don't want to abuse it
I just want to make it up and play it how I choose it.

It was made to be played
Ugly though appealing
Similarities revealing
Looks can be deceiving
If you like the music, then you'll understand the meaning.

It may be different
And the people might not like it
What will they think of it?
Will they understand it?
If it makes no money, will I abandon it?

What should I call my songs
To give the right impression?
Will they gain attention
Or even get a mention?
If I like my music, then need I ask such questions?

Are my ideas the right ideas?
Is this shape a shapeless shape?
Is it gonna make or break?
Either way, how long will it take?
If it doesn't go anywhere, what changes will I have to make?

Just another question before things begin:
Am I really sure about the shape I'm in?
I may not be heavy, but I feel I'm too thin
I'd like to put on weight if things start to begin.

I like writing songs as a form of expression
I like playing music with a hint of aggression
My songs are on paper, my music's on tape
I'd like it on CD but is it the right shape?

Engine With No Wheels

I feel like an engine
I've got time to kill, but I've got no wheels
I feel like an engine
I've got fuel to burn, but no wheels to turn
I feel like an engine, but I've got no wheels.

Like a train with no rails, like an egg without a shell
Like an innocent one in jail — help! Get me out!

The road ahead looks clear, but all I fear
Is when I get things moving all hopes will disappear.

The road I can see, tormenting me
Travelling through my dreams, to reality
Wheels are rolling by, hah! Who am I?
I feel like I'm dying before I've even lived my life.

I feel like an engine, but I've got no wheels.

Guarden was a word that I created. It is an amalgamation of guard and garden.

"Guarden Mind!"

Building up a barrier
They ain't gonna take me away from me
Elders always wanna give too much
They want to run my life.

They've done their time and now it's mine
We've all got a life of our own
It seems they want to change me
And make me their son —
"Guarden Mind!"

Building up a barrier
Independence isn't wrong
We all need space to grow
It's the best way to learn
To be strong
Learn wrong from right
I can plant ideas how and when I like
In the shade, or in the light
Then one day may flourish and bloom…
Not too soon!
I'll sit in my dark room
And wait for the dawning of the day.

I'm living, I'm learning
I'm growing, I'm earning
What one could never give
Experiencing how to live
Without all the hand-me-downs.

Am I cruel?
Cruel to be kind
I'll stick to my lines
Learn in my time
Watch the sunshine…
"Guarden Mind!"

Building up a barrier
No-one's gonna change my ways
Each to their own, for now let me be
Experience of time makes the wise succeed —
"Guarden mind!"

Life's no bed of roses when you're young
That's the way it should be.

'The grass is greener on the other side'
I've heard said many times
I've never agreed with that, to believe

You've gotta be on the other side
Oh, I lied, when one day I found myself
Standing on the other side.

Building up a barrier
Each to their own
Then the next man wouldn't know
What the other had grown —
Each to their own!

We should thrive in our lives
Dwell in our homes
Go alone and live a life of pride —
"Guarden mind!"

The same views are handed down
From generation to generation
We all go our own way
And play with the cards we're dealt
We all do things which we later regret
But that's a part of life.

At the time it's the only way
All advice has no part to play
Regrets maybe made, but that's how the game is played —
"Guarden mind!"

It's a term I use for guarding my views —
"Guarden mind!"

Perseverance

Gotta learn to stay on top of it all
And learn how to get up when you hit the floor
How to brake before you lose control
And how to fight until you reach that goal.

Get-up! Get up and fight
Kick down walls that obscure your sights
Don't ever stop, don't let them stop you
Don't ever stop until you reach the top — keep it up!

Persevere if you want nothing less
Gotta keep pushing for what you think is best.

Self-belief's to be achieved
If you want it you'll get it whatever it is
Aims, goals, desires and dreams
Come together when you've got these things:
Confidence
Determination
Stamina
And a little patience.

Confidence aids self-assurance
Determination leaps all hurdles
Stamina is strength of mind
Patience bares the length of time.

Perseverance is what you need
If you want to succeed
You have got to persevere!

Stick to Your Guns

You waited so long
For the chance to come
To gain recognition
For something you'd done
You were pleased with your work
And what you had achieved
But no-one else
Had the same beliefs.

They said they would like it if they made a few changes
Snip it here, cut it there, slightly rearrange it
But say no, 'cos it's your show
And you should present it how you meant it.

But then you go with the flow
And the people seem to like it
You're convinced at first
When the masses start to buy it
But in years to come
When the people reminisce
All you're remembered for
Is something that you never wished.
Is it an interest, or is it a business?
When interest grows it becomes an investment
It used to be enjoyed, before it was exploited
It's hard to turn back now your mind is disjointed."

Stick to your guns
If you like what you've done
Stick to your guns
Don't change for anyone
Stick to your guns
Don't care about what is
Said by the rest
Just do what you think is best—
Stick to your guns!

It's a Deal

You want time — we'll give you time
You want money — we'll give you money
But if you want success
Then do what you think is best.

You need space — we'll give you space
You want freedom — we'll give you freedom
You want attention, you want recognition
You want the credit which you feel you deserve.

We'll give you all we can, spare you what you need
But if you want to succeed, come on!

Take it away! Let me hear you play
If you're good enough a deal could be made
Play what you want and nothing less
Watch out, here comes success!

"Right, please can you sign here?"

This song is the end of the dream, and the contract is not signed.

Album 2: Lost Property

This was my first album, as The Lost Connection. It was released at the end of 2019. I had recorded over 100 songs and chose these specific songs for this album. It was called 'Lost Property' because it had songs that were suitable only for me to sing, as they were about me or had significant relevance to my life.

1. Simple Man
2. Lost, But Never Forgot
3. Reflect
4. Never Too Old For This Stage
5. No Time To Waste
6. 'All Or Nothing' Kind Of Man
7. "Write-On!" Track
8. Got What I Need
9. Connection
10. Solitary Writer
11. Never Too Late

12. The Lost Waltz Song Poem
13. My Piano Tune Song Poem
14. Nobody Knows
15. This Is How It Is
16. New Tracks
17. Sociable Man
18. My Wishing Well

On this album, the 5th verse was accidently missed out.

Simple Man

I'm a simple man
I know very little about this land
I live my life in a casual fashion
Playing music is my only passion.

I've got no political views
The country is run by the ones others choose
I've got no complaints because I know very little
The country maybe crumbling, but it means nothing to me…My world is sound.

I wouldn't know if the queen died
Or if there was a war outside
I never know who is on strike
I continue doing the things that I like.

The whole world really means nothing to me
Everyone complains about policies,
the economy and redundancies
People's needs always seem to be
What never is.
I let the others who know more
Fight for their rights, stick in their oar
Most of them are angry people
Rowing up a heavy stream.

I'm a simple man
I manage to get by
With what I'm given
I'm able to survive.

Perhaps I'm one of a kind
Blind, with a simple mind
But I've a happy life
Stress free, no strife.

I'm a simple man.

'Lost, But Never Forgot' was a song for which the lyrics and music (including the beat) were all spontaneously created while playing it the keyboard. This was the only time I have written a song in this way.

Lost, But Never Forgot

Another new year, another start
Will it come together or be torn apart?
So now, what I've got
Is a musical background of not a lot
In terms of success
I don't really try to impress
Should I perhaps, from now on
To be where I feel I belong?

So, now this is my plan
To do the best I can
And reveal some of my past
And that is so very vast.

So where do I begin?
I've got loads of tunes and songs to sing
But this is something new
Quite different to what I usually do.
So, will it do well?
Only one way to actually tell
Here it is, for all to hear
Stats will reveal whether it has any appeal.

So now, watch this space
And I hope that I find my place
And be where I wanna be
Somewhere in the music industry
If not, I know I've still got
My backlog of songs that will never be forgot
Lost….
But never forgot.

Reflect

It's time to forget about loved ones
And what people expect
Many live for love
But some live to regret.

It's time to forget about work
And day to day chores
Although some enjoy their jobs
Many find it a bore.

It's time to reflect
Look in the mirror and what do you see?
Life's based around others
But now it's time to think about… me!

Create a space in your mind
A space just for you
And find some time to unwind
And do what you wanna do.

Once you've created space
Free from despair
You may go a little crazy
Because space these days is rare.

Once you've freed your mind
You've got space to create
Something that is yours
And, in time, we can all share."

Look and reflect, in time, respect
What no-one else can see
With space in time, what's in your mind
Can be enjoyed by everybody.

Never Too Old for This Stage

Baby lying crying
Boy and his toy
Teenager in danger
A strange sense of joy
Twenties now and ageing
Moving stage by stage
The book becomes deeper
Turn another page.

Win, lose —
A sense of confusion
Turn another page…
Nothing lost.

The past has gone
But remains
Here comes the future —
Time to gain.

Never too old, never lost
What is the cost of life?

Gain tomorrow, lose today
Then another slips away
What is the price of life, hey?

Time is free, without request
Collect or reject, what comes next?
Look left, look right
Know where you stand
Feel an inner kick
Subconscious command
Demand something more
Than what you've got.

Turning grey, never mind,
There's no limit we should find
Success may become one day
Gone tomorrow...

Easy come, easy go
High and low in every place
When you're down — you know, you learn
How dreams can earn
Tomorrow...
Soon to be yesterday.

Memories...
Then one day you die — why?
What's the price of life, hey?

Never too old for this stage.

No Time to Waste

When people look at me, what they see
Is someone who is very fast
It seems I'm living on borrowed time
And tomorrow is my last.

And when I work, I'm berserk, I'm a blur
But when on a bonus it pays
And now I've set a precedence
It's harder to change my ways.

It's in my blood, it's in my genes
I don't mean to rush, although it seems
If I could, I would go slow
But it's not in my nature though.

In my spare time, when it's fine
I play golf in a strange fashion
I'm chasing the ball before it lands
But I play with vigour and passion.

But when it comes to decisions
That will be remembered in time
Which will influence my future
I'm in a different frame of mind.

But now we're over the bridge
It's pedal to the metal.

And as I drive, living life in a rush
I don't want to get stuck in the queues
The quicker I get from here to there
The less time that I lose —
No time to waste!

'All or Nothing' Kind of Man

When feeling tired and worn
And I can't perform to the max'
I feel it's best just to chill out
Sit back and relax.

I'm an 'all or nothing' kind of man
When I'm good I'm flying, without even trying
But when I'm not, not tip-top
I stop.

I used to be a die-hard
And battle through pain
My relentless endeavour
Was a credit to my name.

In the past I persisted
But I've learnt to draw the line
I set too high a precedence
And was taken for granted all the time.

If I'm not 100%
When I say no, that's what I meant
In the past backwards I've bent
But no more 'cos that I resent.

I'm an 'all or nothing' kind of man
I'm all or nothing, that's what I am
'All or nothing' kind of man.

'Write-On!' Track

I write about rights, and I write about wrongs
I'm right on track when I'm writing these songs
I write about life, and I write about death
I write so when I've gone something is left.

I'll just speak 'cos I can't really sing
Perhaps just rapping is my kind of thing
I tend to rely on the tune and the beat
To make you hum or move your feet.

Right on! Let's big-up the beat
Right on! Let's turn up the tune
Are you now moving your feet
Or digging this sound in your room?

I write, I write, I write
I'm back *(Write on!)*
I'm writing another track…
I'm right on track!

Got What I Need

When I'm at home, on my own
When I'm alone in my home
Don't need anyone for fun
For fun I don't need anyone
Got what I need.

I feel the need for something more
Something more I feel I need
But I have everything already
I already have everything
Got what I need.

Sometimes I feel the need to be greedy
But no need — I'm far from needy
Really, no need to rely on anyone
If I am strong, I can please myself
Mentally and in health
Be healthy and through fortune
Life will decide if I'm to become fortunate
And wealthy, but ultimately
Happiness is all I need
To declare success.
I must confess
That now and again
I get stressed
And feel a sense of loneliness
And become depressed
But only because
Society makes me feel
Like an outcast!
But loneliness is happiness.

When I'm at home, on my own
Don't need anyone for fun
Because I've got what I need
Got what I need!

Connection

Some things come to light
The more you see, the more you grow to like
Some things look good
But are they really? Is it really understood?

If understood
What comes to be
You will find, is a connection of the minds
It's all about personality.

It's a matter of taste
We're all unique, we must appreciate
Looks are deceiving
Look at my face — am I worth believing in?
I rest my case!

To look and relate
All based on face value
But a note in one's ear
Then I know you will hear, and see
A connection and my friend
It may never end.

Solitary Writer

As a writer, I write what I feel
What anyone thinks is no big deal
I've got my feelings, I've got my views
I write what I like, I write what I choose.

I look for meaning, I like to express
The results I find may not impress
But in my space, I feel at ease
Warm in my house alone, but outside I'll freeze.

I am a solitary writer
Much of me is concealed
But on paper all is revealed
What you see ain't what you get
What I write you don't expect.

I'm not the same, when alone
I transform when in the zone
I'm known as crazy and a bit of a nightmare
But in my space, I'm a solitary writer.

I may seem happy, but usually I'm sad
My life is okay, but I feel bad
I succeed in life, but it's not really me
Doing what I don't want to, and never feeling free.

Paying the bills — just a nobody
I need my dream world to become a reality.
Be what I wanna be and not what I don't
The time has come to grab my life by the throat
And squeeze hard until it chokes
And shake it up!

Kill the night, enhance the dawn
And in the light of day
A new life will be born.

'Never Too Late' was based on somebody I knew, who was about 60 years old. After writing about him I thought a lot of it sounded similar to me, so I changed it to 50. Not all the details are relative to me, but the sentiment of the song was something I could relate to.

Never Too Late

He was alone all his life
Had no kids and had no wife
He slept days and worked all night
Socially it wasn't right.

But for him it seemed okay
Became a loner set in his ways
He worked hard and he saved well
A rich man, but you couldn't tell.

Then, when he reached 50
He opened his mind and he could see
Time passing by and the end drawing near
In his mind it was clear.

Time to break free from routine
Let go and live the dream
A fortune he'd earned and now time to spend
Took a while for him to comprehend
But now he finally had.

Never too late for you to change
For the best, but it might be strange
You only live once and then you're done
You're not a machine — make time for fun.

These are lyrics that were written to a tune which I created in 1990, while having piano lessons. Nearly 3 decades later I decided to turn the tune into a song (or poem in this case)

The Lost Waltz Song Poem

Music is sweet, music's bizarre
Rap is in, but lacking guitar
Music's unlimited, anything goes
Ideas are endless and it shows.

When I play in a different way
I forget trends, what can I say?
Whatever style enters my head
Is what it is, don't care what is said.

It maybe disliked but I don't care
But I am happy still to share.

This is 'The Lost Waltz'
My reason for failure is my own fault
Against the normal I tend to revolt.

These are the words to a tune
From a long time ago
And so now my music's become
As well as a tune — a poem, a song.
This was a tune which I also created, while having piano lessons. It took over 2 decades to finally get around to adding lyrics to it and recording it as a song.

My Piano Tune Song Poem

I never ever wanted to find fame
I never wanted to have a known name
I can't deny that I wanted success
But more for myself, but it's nice to impress.

I started off talentless
Not very skilled, but had creativity
I tried to learn the proper way
But my creativity led me astray.

I managed to move my fingers around the keys
And lyrically I was good, so songs came to be
I only hoped that one day…
I'd be able to sing.

Nobody Knows

It's strange to hear
What people think of me
What they think I am
And what I should be.

Psychiatrists maybe clever
But not clever enough
We could talk for years
And it still wouldn't be enough.

Nobody knows
Nobody knows me
You can see me; you can hear me
You can talk to me too
But you'll never know me
Like I don't know you.

*I tried to update an old tune and make it sound more modern,
but that didn't quite happen on 'This Is How It Is'.*

This Is How It Is

Things in the past will always last
And the dreams we have we try to keep
But through the course of time
We can't often find what we seek.

So, from the past, it's time to shine
And rise instead of sink
Try and keep in touch with the real world
Time to rethink.

This is the way it is, now
I'm not sure of myself
Got to think positive about how I live
Listen, learn and improve
To make a difference
And this is how it is.

A part of the past, brought to the future
Can I communicate, or is it too late?
I need to connect, instead of feeling lost
And perhaps a change maybe worth the cost
And this is how it is.

*This was about trying to become the
young creative person I used to be.*

New Tracks

Times are changing
They're changing fast
Things are always changing
Nothing ever lasts
We've gotta move on
Leave it all behind
Gotta try and find
Things in life
That can't cause us pain
Learn from the past
In the future we may gain
That something which we lack
The only way is forward
And there ain't no turning back —
It's time to lay down new tracks.

The old me knew me, the new me lost touch
He got lost in love, then run out of luck
Now I am back, living more carefree
But what you see ain't always the whole story
We suffer pain in hope to find glory —
That which we lack
The only way is forward and there ain't no turning back
It's time to lay down new tracks.

The old me got in touch
Before I was engaged
He said, *"Life shouldn't be
determined by age"*.

So then I turned back and took the old route
I was in pursuit of a life that was true to me
Lost for a while but regained, eventually
The personality which I lacked
Now I'm going forward after turning back
Now I'm replacing (*yes!*)
I'm renewing the old tracks.

The old me knew me better
The old me — new me now
The old me knew me better
To remain this way I vow.

Album 3: 2020 Vision

This album was about the year 2020. COVID-19 had a major influence on the whole of this album, although some of the lyrics were written many years and decades before. It was the year where I gained more of a vision and perspective as to what I really needed in life.

1. Life (We Live, Learn And Die)
2. It's My Medication
3. Drive
4. 2020 Vision
5. One Big Army
6. Captain Tom
7. Love
8. While Furloughed
9. Two Shades Of Blue
10. Between Dreams And Reality
11. Voluntary Redundancy

12. Freedom Seeker
13. 'In The Middle' Kind Of Man
14. Guilt Tripping On Happiness
15. A Maze In Life
16. In Time We Will Succeed
17. All Stars (Shine On!)
18. The Key To Eternity
19. Time Will Tell

Life (We Live, Learn and Die)

Life is a fusion
Of imagination and disillusion
The first answers we find
We see when we're half blind
All the results then widen our vision…
The vision that creates our minds.

Events that we see
From varying degrees
Pictures of the scenes of the things that have been
Reflected on the minds as focussed through the eyes
The eyes that create our guise…
And lives.

Facts are intrusions
On our earlier forgone conclusions
Once focussing on the ground
But now looking all around
The more our results, the more we make decisions
Decisions, decisions…
Decisions that decide our fate
Life — we live, learn and die.

It's My Medication

We earn to spend
We eat to be fed
We look to see
Listen to hear what is said
But…

Sometimes, things don't make sense
Confusing, frustrating
Need educating
Is it them, or you or me?
Eye to eye we cannot see
Turn away, block all vision
Accept difference and division
Slip into another dimension
My escape's my medication.

Think, write, think sound
Think outside the common ground
Think, write, escape, break
Where it leads to is what it takes…
It's medicinal
It's my medication!

Drive

Got the engine running
It's time to do something
Get the wheels rolling
Don't know where we're going yet.

When we get moving
We'll be cruising along
And something will show
Ready, steady, let's go!

Now in the driving seat
Going forward, time to meet
Whatever we decide
But for now, we'll just drive.

Foot down
No hanging around
Moving at last
Into the vast.

Looking out
Seeing what's about
If nothing catches the eye
Just enjoy the ride.

At this point we'll slow down
Pullover, what have we found?
What do we need? Have we arrived?
Should we plot a route
Or just continue to drive?

Whatever comes, comes
Whatever goes, goes
But, when in the driving seat
We can decide what we meet
And when the journey is complete
It's time to jump back
Into the driving seat
And drive!

2020 Vision

New year once again
Another end, another start
A new outlook, a new decade
New decisions to be made
And action to be took.

New year once again
Time to amend and improve
We're making major moves
Brexit has now finally been approved
Leaving the EU maybe strange
But it's time for change.

Times are changing
For better or worse
Climate change is still a threat
Floods and fires to expect
Ozone layer's diminishing, or in self-repair?
Will the world unite or fight?
We live in fear.

2020 vision — things are so clear
2020 Vision — clearly a mystery
Will things develop, or decline?
'2020 Vision' in my mind
What will be will be…
2020 Vision — c'est la vie.

One Big Army (Verses COVID-19)

We grieve for the deceased
And pray for the dying
One big army
Together we are trying
To stay alive
Hoping to succeed
Doing what we need
To enable recovery.

It takes a tragedy
For universal harmony
One big army
No longer enemies
Fighting in unity
Battling atrocity
To continue to exist
And maintain humanity.

A deadly enemy
An undercover killer
Invisible to the eye (until it gets inside)
Can only protect (and deal with the effects).
This world may never beat it
But hopefully we won't be defeated
And survive until it finally
Retreats and fades away.

But when we recover, we'll need each other still
To rebuild the industries and maintain stability
But will everything change? Will we be better people?
Or be the same as we used to be?

Will gang wars still occur?
Death through murder, poverty and theft?
D and D behaviour, Saturday fatalities
Marriage and divorce and adultery?

Hopefully, life will become
Better for everyone
In the end.

Social distancing creates long queues
Online shopping's easier to do
And how many people will continue to?
More so than before, probably.

Holidays abroad, even if we can afford
Maybe a thing of the past
Especially in regard to business trips
Instead, use zoom on the internet.

But if the internet goes wrong
What will then become?
Will life be better or worse
In the long run?

We're at war, but not with each other
One big army aiding recovery
In whatever capacity
That we can.

But what is the future plan?
For now, we live in limbo
And manage to do
The best that we can.

*This is about Tom Moore. Who became a sir when he reached
100 years old, in 2020.*

Captain Tom

Young Tom Moore was an officer in the war
Back in '39
Serving Queen and country while in the army
On the front-line.

Never been a man like him before
Captain Tom Moore
Never been a man like him before
That is for sure.

"Tomorrow will be a better day"
Tom would always say
He hadn't an easy life, but managed to survive
For over a century.

An achiever, a fighter, a giver, a survivor
Full of positivity
It's fair to say and I'm sure you'll agree
Captain Tom lives forever in our hearts
And in history.
He gained love from far, wide and above
What he ever dreamed
He's just a family man, doing the best he can
But the future was greater than it seemed.

He's a hero of our time
Modest and honest and Tom we promise
You will be remembered
Forever and ever in time.

Love

Friendship is good
But love is dramatic
A life changing feeling
That can be so fantastic
Never know it's coming
But know when it shows
It can't be ignored
Like a seed it will grow.

When it arrives
The more you'll desire
Love is a drug
That burns like a fire
Fire gives warmth
Comfort and energy
But it can burn
And become an enemy.

Love takes you high
But can take you low
Great when it's present
But painful when it goes.
Love, oh love
Is a wonderful thing
Creating emotions
Nothing else can bring.

While Furloughed

It was *'goodbye'*
From me to you
Time to go
The high that was
May never ever show again my friend
Now we are furloughed.

Now we hide
Away inside
Caged apart
We do to survive
A mental test — urges suppressed
Now we are furloughed.

Distanced
Segregated
Trapped inside
Frustrated
But safe alone in our homes
We can communicate by mobile phones, only
Now we are furloughed.

2020
Was looking good
Plans were finally going to plan
How they should
But now we're reflecting
On what could be, or maybe not…
While we are furloughed.

Thoughts had grown
Feelings remained
But deep down inside
We were going insane
Captive, but free from danger and fear
But too far from near, until we reappear
From furlough.

Normal isn't normal
Nothing is clear
Reality isn't really
Real anymore
We live in hope, but hope cannot give
What we need to cope and live
While we are furloughed.

Will we ever see
The very end
Of this pandemic
My friend?
Apart we stay in our bubbles
We grow apart, not knowing anything
While furloughed.

Two Shades of Blue

Two shades of blue
When I think of you
In regard to us
What are we to do?
It's like an ocean —
An adventure, or a view?

When apart, I'm sad and dry
When together we could get wet
Feel the urge to enter
Or live with regret.

Two shades of blue
Feelings I have for you
Together I think deep
Apart it's just a memory…

Without, no doubt
I feel like singing the blues
Clouds appear, but when you're near
There's better things to do.

The outlook is brighter
Feel good inside
Wanna jump on in
When you're by my side.

Desire craves for more
A different blue than before —
Two shades of blue.

Between Dreams and Reality

People say I'm crazy
Just living in a dream
But life isn't always
Quite as easy as it seems
So are my dreams crazy?
Am I crazy after all?
Maybe, or more so
Maybe not at all.

To think realistic
Isn't realistic at all
I'll continue dreaming
Whether regarded as a fool.

I feel you've got to reach out
Reach for your desires
Forget those who knock you
Keep aiming for things higher.

The strange thing is
While living in my dreams

It all seems apparent
And is now happening.

For better or worse
Dreams come first
And the good will always shine through.

Nearly there —
I'm gonna see it through
Until it's reality
And my dreams become true.

I had already planned to write a song about voluntary redundancy if it was granted. It became a major part of the 2020 Vision and my future progress. An extra verse has been added for this book.

Voluntary Redundancy

Time for a decision
A big one to make
Take the money and run
Could be a mistake
Head into the unknown
Or stay where I am?
But things are now changing
So, this is my plan:

Time for a change
Time for pastures new
Find something better
For me to do
But where shall I go?
And what should I do?

My decision's made
I signed on the line
Time to move on
And utilise my time
To find what I need
A better life for me
Time to find myself
And where I should be.

May need a little help,
Is there anybody there
Who can show me the way?
I have time to spare
I have money saved
But no real income
I need to spend wisely
And not regret what I've done.

Voluntary redundancy
Because I need a break
A black hole in the blue
Could be a great escape
It's something I've gotta do
A chance I've gotta take.

Freedom Seeker

I wanna go
To places that I've never known
I wanna see
Things that I'll never be shown
You only live once, gotta take a chance
Can't wait for it to come
No good dreaming if it's something you believe in
It's gotta be done
From the cage I'm on the run.

I'm gonna get out
And find what it's all about
Gonna experience feelings
That I've never felt

Life's a test and you need to progress
And find what you wish you had
Need to be glad, don't wanna be sad
So, I'm looking for fun
From the cage I'm on the run.

I'm seeking freedom
I'm a freedom seeker
Life to me seems bleak, unless I go out to seek
Freedom.

You can call me a cynic, but it's how I see it
When stuck in the cog wheels of time and space
In the working place — the only time I show my face
No time for anything, so things have gotta change.

The working life's fine,
But I feel it isn't mine
Feels like I'm doing time
Living like the sun shines.

I've gotta move, gotta prove
That I'm not stuck in a groove
So I feel the time has come
From the cage I'm on the run.

This is an updated version of 'All Or Nothing' Kind Of Man song, using the same chords and riff.

'In the Middle' Kind of Man

Nothing too little and nothing too much
In the middle and never lose touch
With my finger in every pie
I can remain a happy guy.

I am the man in the middle
I am an 'in-the-middle' kind of man.

Nothing too shallow and nothing too deep
Simple pleasure is all I seek
And now I just go with the flow
With whatever comes or goes.

In the past I was OTT
And ended-up where I didn't wanna be
Now I'm glad to be where I'm at
And can say as a matter of fact.

I'm a man of leisure, not greed
And on pleasure I now feed
Want no more than what I've got
Got what I need to hit the spot.

I am now the man in the middle
Know when to shoot and when to dribble
Now no troubles, my life is in tact
I'll score when I need to have an impact.

I am ready whenever, and wherever
And however that maybe.

I am the man in the middle
I am an 'in-the-middle' kind of man, yes I am.

Guilt Tripping on Happiness

Now that I feel happy within
I get a guilt trip, I can't win
I feel like a sinner, once I was a winner
It's hard to be happy in a world that is sad
That's life — too bad!
I'm guilt tripping on happiness.

Guilt's getting heavy and it's pulling me
Into a depression, my mind's in recession
I was having fun, it was annoying everyone
Jealousy of joy — a bitter world's become.

Happiness is loathed by the sad
They've forgot what it is to be glad
And so, I went from high to low
And that is how the story goes
I guilt tripped and now I am just another
Sad git!

I'm guilt tripping on happiness.

A Maze in Life

I'm in a maze
Don't know which way to go
Which way should I turn?
No openings seem to show.

I've gone down many roads
That lead to dead ends
All I seem to be doing
Is going around the bend.

Some say life's amazing
It's a maze in life
Will I ever escape
Or forever be trapped inside?

Some say life's amazing
But not so much for me
I'm trapped in the middle
Of not where I should be.

Life — it's a maze in
Life — it's doing my head in
Life — don't know where to begin
Get me out of this maze I'm in.

'In Time We Will Succeed' was written after 7 years of very little creative activity. This was originally called 'Spare Time' and appeared on the album 'Time Is Running Out', released by Innovator (the rock band I was in) as a collaborative song. In 2017 I left Innovator and decided to record the song as I originally intended, but with new words so it wasn't too similar to 'Spare Time' anymore.

In Time We Will Succeed

Spare time goes to waste
Stuck in a rut, in the same place
Going nowhere and lacking in drive
Sit around moaning about everything in life.

We need a break, or we'll break down
New things need to be found
We seem to have lost the will to progress
All efforts seem to lead to stress.

We need to see who we are
What we are and can be
Enjoy what we do, gain belief and achieve
And through happiness, succeed.

In time, prevent decline
Less TV and use our minds
Start to think and create
Life's too short to hesitate.
Let's start to motivate
Brain engage, get in the mood
It's time for all of us to prove
Life can be good.

Another day and I fear
That the end is drawing near
Got to stop and think clear
Things ain't as bad as they appear.

Look back at what we enjoyed
Revitalise if not destroyed
What was good we shouldn't avoid
All hopes should be deployed.

Spare time we should embrace
And time never ever waste
If fed up, refuel desire
The more we do, the less we tire.

Now we look back in time
And this is what we find
What has gone can now come back
When we discover what we lack.

We need to see who we are
What we are and can be
Enjoy what we do, gain belief and achieve
And through happiness, succeed.

All Stars (Shine On!)

We're all stars in our own right
Some just shine a brighter light
Some can't be seen
But they're somewhere in the night.

We're all stars but so far
No-one's seen who we are
We hide in the depths of time
But shine from afar.

We seem to be like mites
Tiny specks of light
But are distant forms of energy
Far greater and more bright.

We're all stars and keep shining
In ourselves we are surviving
We'll stay high and will keep trying
Until we shoot and gone —
Shine on!

Key to Eternity

I'm tired of analysing life
Like many, more than any myself
We all ask the question, 'Why are we here?'
We'll be asking forever, and it still won't be clear.

The meaning of life is a big mystery
But now we are here, understand
That realisation of utilisation
Of the resources we have, or are given, is a must.

And I'm sure and I trust
That we've learnt from the past
And that love holds the key
To the door of eternity.

Time Will Tell

I'm a man on a mission
With a 2020 vision
Smiling with adversity
No-one can understand
No-one can see
What's going on in my mind
No-one but me.

New world
New beginnings
New outlook
Big decisions
Which only I can make
But sometimes in life
The chances you've gotta take.

If all fails
I can handle that
With failure I'm familiar
As a matter of fact

Sitting on the fence
Misses opportunities
But I ain't gonna do something
That ain't really me.

I'd rather fail
Doing what creates pleasure
Than succeeding at something
That's a meaningless endeavour
Playing safe in first gear
With time and money
My vision is clear.

Time will tell
If right or wrong
It's not about where I am
It's about where I belong
The destination is close
The journey was long
Time will tell
The time is now very soon.

Album 4: The New Lost World 19-20-21

During and after COVID-19, life changed in so many ways, for me especially. While taking a break from work, I paid for a 6-month online sync-writing course. During this period, I learnt more about music technology and my own musical equipment and recording techniques. I listened to pros in the music industry, wrote music and songs to briefs (as assignments), collaborated with people around the world. When I combined these tasks with my own viewpoint and circumstances, these songs were recorded between 2019 to 2021, although some of the lyrics were written as long ago as 1990. It was released on 1-9-2021.

1. Rain On Me
2. Love In A Lower Key
3. Sunshine Mind

4. It's A New Day
5. Now I'm With You
6. Back To Work
7. Voices In My Head
8. I'm A Rebel
9. I Am Your Guiding Light
10. Winning Team
11. At The Top
12. Too Much!
13. The 'Great' Rap Track
14. Mr Retro

'Rain On Me' was originally recorded as 'Drought', when I used water to symbolise love. This version was sung by a lady from South Africa, who was on the same sync-writing course as me, but using a more simplistic chord sequence.

Rain on Me

I feel so alone
I've got nobody, I'm on my own
As I lie here crying
It feels like I'm dying
It feels as though I'm sinking in the sand.

I feel incomplete
Too unstable for my feet
As I lie on the ground
I feel I'll drown
It feels like I'm drowning in the air.

Do you understand how I feel?
It feels so unreal
Without anybody
Without the one I love
Heavens above —
Rain on me.

My wish when I die
Is I'll rise to the sky
To the heavenly pools ascend
To unite once again
But for now, my love lies on the wind.

Do you understand how I feel?
I feel I won't heel
Now I'm alone
Without the one I loved
Heavens above —
Rain on me.

Love in a Lower Key

I don't wanna get too serious
Serious leads to stress and pain
Unless it is serious fun
For which then I am fair game.

Fun is fun, if kept in the lower key
Enjoy it while you can
If things get serious
Make them understand.

I like to keep it short and sweet
With every woman that I meet
I like the warmth, but when it gets too hot
I get too weak and lose the plot
Need to keep it in the lower key.

I like to thrill and boredom avoid
Avoid the dwindling pleasure
When it's new, excitement is high
But probably not forever.

Don't wanna get too high on love
I want a lift, but just enough
To bring me back to life
But not too much, that isn't right for me
So I want love to be
Kept in a lower key

Sunshine Mind

When I woke today
I didn't feel okay
Just doom and gloom
But had time to think
I'll stay on top
Weather good or not
I've always got sunshine in my mind.

Clouds will clear
Just a matter of time
I have no fear
And I'll keep in mind
Bright times will always appear.

Beneath I know
But it doesn't show
My eyes disguise
What you can't see
Down below
Beneath my skin
I know eventually I will win.

The sun exists
It never goes away
Sunshine all the time
Even when it's grey
New day soon
Amidst the gloom
Yesterday is history
Brighter things will always come to be.

We all have sunshine
Sunshine in the mind
Winds may blow
Storms may show
But behind, I know
I'll always have sunshine in my mind.

It's a New Day

It's a new world
It's a new way
It's a new life
It's a new day

It's a new day

It's a new day

It's a new day!

'Now I'm With You' was written soon after meeting and becoming Debbie's partner.

Now I'm with You

Life can be hard
But we've gotta get through
Keep a positive mind
It's something we've gotta do.

Bad things may happen
Which we cannot control
We deal with the situation
And onto hope we try to hold.

Things can be good
But change before we know
But when times are bad
Better things will show.

And for me it's true to say
Much misfortune has come my way
But then suddenly from out of the blue
A complete turnaround occurred
When I met you.

New hope in the face of fear
A new beginning and the future is clear
Suddenly, I'm where I want to be
Now I'm with you…

And you
Are
With me.

Back to Work

I took a break
A great escape
Time to think
Decisions to make
Many changes
And things to do
New discoveries
I'm learning too.

But now
I've gotta face the fact
Money's needed
I've gotta get back to work…
To work.

I took a break
I needed a rest
But my bank balance
Is now much less.

I'm going back to work.

I am often in two minds. One wants to progress and the other doesn't trust venturing out of his comfort zone.

Voices in My Head

I've got voices in my head
Saying: *"Don't see green only see red*
Don't go forward, go back instead"
Don't know if to believe what is said
By these voices in my head.

I've got voices in my head
Saying different things, can't believe what I'm fed
But the dumb side may know better instead
Amber light flashing
I'm in-between green and red…
With these voices going 'round in my head.

This was written to the theme of 'rebel' — which was another task set on the course I was on. This is not about anyone in particular, but is very similar to me in some respects.

I'm a Rebel

I never seem to be able to conform
My way of thinking isn't that of the norm'
It's not my problem, you've got to understand
It's just the way I am — I'm a rebel.

All advice and rules I don't need
To be an individual and succeed
With the majority I'm not in sync'
I'm an individual — for myself I can think.

I'm a rule breaker, rules break me
It's the only way for me to be me —
I'm a rebel.

I don't care about looks and don't follow trends
I ain't a cool guy and I haven't many friends
I do what I like and I like what I do
I'm here to please me and not please you.
I don't mean to offend, on me I must depend —
I'm a rebel
Decisions I make, the chances I take —
I'm a rebel.

Although I'm a rebel
I'm a rebel with a level head
I'm a rebel on a mission
But with vision instead.

I'm a rule breaker, rules break me
It's the only way for me to be me —
I'm a rebel

This is about the positive side of a person, trying to motivate their lazier, negative side.

I Am Your Guiding Light

You don't know what you've got to do
You don't know who to turn to
Most of the time you're just scratching your head
Some days you don't even want to get out of bed.

But you've got to try and get a grip
Pull yourself together — don't let yourself slip
Into a place you don't want to be
Get into gear and come with me.

I am the one inside
I am the one from which you hide
When I find you, you just wanna fight
But I am your guiding light.

This was written for the collaborative team I was in on the sync-writing course. Nobody took on the lyrics, so I did it all myself.

Winning Team

I meet you
You meet me
We meet them
And come to be
A group
A team
With similar aims
And similar dreams.

A common thread brought us here
With a passion overriding fear
On a mission, we'll strike a chord
And collectively reap reward.

We have desire
Together a force
Together united
And in due course

Success will become
Together we're strong
And we are now
Where we belong.

Together in harmony
Creating positivity
No negativity
In good company
And where
We were always meant to be.

We are a winning team
Full of hope and self-esteem
We are a winning team
Now reality is the dream.

Another task was set, to write about someone who was at the top of their game, and this was the result soon after.

At the Top

*I'm here at the top
With drive I drove, along winding roads
Up and down, with highs and lows
But I never stopped.*

*I'm here at the top
On slopes I slipped, but I got a grip
Determined and dedicated
To get me where I've got.*

*Now here I'm pleased to be
Power earned through things I learnt
With grand expectations
This world now depends on me.*

*As a winner I'm worthy
Of servants and slaves
Palace and parades
Here before me
I'm not majestic
I'm a worker that doesn't work
Like I did before
But I am rich
And much more powerful.*

*But is this the figure
That I wanted to be?
I feel I have the weight
Of the world upon me
I may be in control —
I rose above you all
I am at the top…*

But when will I fall?

Too Much

Oh, to be a millionaire
Too much!
Live life without a care
Too much!
Live it up
All the time
That kind of thing ain't good for the mind.

Oh, to be a superstar
Too much!
Wherever you go the press ain't far
Too much!
Enjoy what you do
And the money's great
But plenitude can lead to negative fate.

Success — call it such
But I'd like to keep in touch
With the inner me
I am glad to be
The little man that I am…
Just enough.
Oh, to be a sex symbol
Too much!
Gotta look nice and act so cool
Too much!
It may be good to be admired by many
But as for love lives, they haven't had any.

Millionaires, superstars
Sex symbols — whoever you are
Do you enjoy what you have become?
Or have things gone too far?
Do you enjoy what you've become
Or who you are?

Too much!

This was called, 'Great' and written in 1995. The music was created for a hip-hop brief and these lyrics were selected to go with it. The brief deadline ended before the song was completed. This is when I decided to add extra lyrics.

The 'Great' Rap Track

The greatest things in life
Are actually quite small
The greatest things are great in size
But not that great at all
They lose their appeal
Things get out of hand
Shapes become shapeless shapes
As they continue to expand.

It's not the size that counts, they say
But the bigger the better's the order of the day
It's always seemed to have been that way
But I disagree.

Small is cool, but out of sight
It's kept preserved, but not conserved
It's kept untouched and wild and free
So the bigger the better's not for me.
It's great! — greatly overrated
When you hear it every day
You either grow to love or hate it
As you can see it's not for me
Clever minds with commercial inclines
I'm not inclined to follow these lines
Using time to shine and please
Just for money is a sign of greed
Notes for notes on the music scene
Controlling minds in the scheme of things
Saying things that are cool and hip, hop, skip, trip, trap.

It's great! It's great! — It's greatly overrated
When you hear it every day you either grow to love
or hate it
Cunning minds with commercial inclines
Devious plans of the dictating kind
Power of sound in our heads
We see what we hear, and feed on what we're fed…
But I see red!

Not out to preach, dictate or guide
Just gotta let you decide.

The greatest things in life
Are actually quite small
The greatest things are great in size
But not that great at all.

Mr Retro

They call him Mr Retro
He drives an Austin Metro
Born in the village
Not in a ghetto.

Born a black bloke
He lived in a cloud of smoke
Close to the 'henge
Stone days never end.

Wearing his flared jeans
They call him Mr. Retro
Jimi Hendrix on headphones
Placed on his afro.

A boy in the 70s
Grew up in the 80s
Adult in the 90s
He lived life carefree
He loved the 60s

More than the noughties
And then when he reached 40
He suddenly changed.

He met a white girl
Much younger, but old enough
And made him see things differently
And listen to different stuff.

This was a trip
But he was there for the long ride
Different interests they had
Brought them closer, rather than divide.

Album 5: Whatever Happened

This album has the songs that made this book become a complete story. 'The one thing I needed to feel I've succeeded, and continue to, is...' [sic} explained in the lyrics of 'You'. Sometimes, you just need to find the right pieces at the right times, for good things to happen.

1. Won't Stop!
2. Shattering
3. (Feel The Vibe) With This Tribe
4. Ifs And Buts
5. I Am Just Me
6. The Fastest Man In The World
7. I Don't Like What I Do
8. The Best
9. Golden Anniversary
10. Beep! Beep!
11. Hot Dog
12. What Is Justice?
13. You
14. Forever Together, Me And You
15. We Won't Stop!

'Won't Stop' was created out of chords that my friend and I jammed back in the late 80s or 90s. After I wrote lyrics to the two chord patterns, I mentioned what I had done, and my mate agreed to help update it. 'Won't Stop' has a new solo section, with the chords my friend suggested. When time allowed, we got back together and finally recorded an updated version, with a slightly different structure and added lyrics, to make it a truly collaborative effort.

Won't Stop!

(A brief extract that wasn't in the 2nd version on the album, called 'We Won't Stop!')

We won't stop!
Even if you say 'stop'
We won't stop, won't stop.

In 2014, I recorded 'Cracks', but never released it. Jodylynn Telavi, in 2021, was looking for dark music, with a simplistic riff, to work on. I presented my music to her and these lyrics were the result. They were written by me, but with suggestions and guidance from Jodylynn.

Shattering

I feel imprisoned
Walls are closing in
Pressure's growing
Hopes are wearing thin.

Can you feel it?
Can you see it shattering?

Cracks I can feel
Cracks I can see
Cracks appearing
Between you and me.

We were free
Solid as a rock
The situation changed
Normality just stopped.
We try so hard
To keep it together
And prevent
Whatever
Shattering!

Cracks I can feel
I can see
Cracks between you and me.

I feel it
I see it
Shattering!

'(Feel The Vibe) With My Tribe' came about after receiving a brief. Music was needed for a film about some young people travelling from island to island on a boat, in an adventure about discovering and learning new things (if I recall rightly). Its creation begun in a collaborative group of 3, but the song was not finished in time to meet the deadline. I changed all the words and, as I was the creator of the music, nobody had any qualms about me owning the song 100%.

(Feel the Vibe) With This Tribe

I feel alive
I feel so free
I need these guys
To be with me.

I'm never down
When they're around
I come to life
With this sound.

I was alone
An empty zone
I reached out
To the unknown.

Then when
I did, I found
My people
On a common ground.

Dance, dance, dance, dance!
Let's do the tribal dance!

Got desire
And fire
With this tribe
Get higher
Got the vibe
Got the feel
With this tribe
Life is real.

A challenge was set, to write a song in which the main word was, 'If'. Within 24 hours I had written words and had recorded it as a complete song.

Ifs and Buts

The places we lived, the people we loved
Could be different for us
If we had talked when we saw, spoke when we met
Instead, we ignored and then lived with regret.

The places we worked, the places we went
Could be different
If we'd spent our time with each other
But instead we fell for the wrong kind of lovers.

How did we never come to be?
Landed ourselves in bad company
Would've treated you well
But too late to tell now.

We can't turn back
Let's put it all behind
There is still time
Memories may remain
But let's blank out the pain
But only if you want me to
Be with you.

No more ifs and buts!

This was written as a person who had tried to gain money to help fulfil his dreams but, instead, lost money to con-artists and scammers. This caused paranoia and negativity to set in.

I Am Just Me

If I can't be me, who can I be?
I can't be you 'cos that ain't true
I can't be better, despite endeavour
I'm just me — whatever!

I am just me
Nothing more I can be
I've done my best
Had little success
But my mission
Was never to impress
So I remain nothing
More or less.

I gave all I got
But didn't get
I like to please
But haven't yet.
The quest to prosper
The urge to gain
A waste of time and money
So I remain 'Lost' forever.

I've done so much
But lost my touch
My brain is drained
My trust is bruised
Losers are winners
And I feel used
Am I stupid?
Paranoid and confused?

Life goes on
Try to be strong
Don't feel quite right
Although I long
To feel better
But never the same
Life is a lesson
It's a shame…

I am just me!

Happiness doesn't have to come from being successful, rich and famous. And this is what 'The Fastest Man…' was based on.

The Fastest Man in the World

The fastest man in the world
Didn't want to race
He knew he was the fastest
And this knowledge he embraced.

People tried to force him
Into competition
He didn't feel the need
So he stuck to his decision.

He felt good inside
And the fact that no-one knew
Wasn't really an issue
Nothing he needed to do.

There was no reason to prove
The speed at which he ran
He was comfortably employed
A fit and healthy man.
He knew he was the fastest
He lived a pleasant life
He had no need for fame
He didn't need the strife.

He wanted no attention
Enjoyed his privacy
No need for recognition
Unknown he could be.

He had a caring woman
He was a caring man
To be anything more
Was never his plan.

People despised him
Said it was a waste
To have such a talent
That never ever raced.

Two trains of thought
Neither's right or wrong
Contention is self-pleasing
But temptation can be strong

Proving you're the best
Is unnecessary
It's the knowing that counts
But some may say:
"To the contrary."

Happiness is cool
But fame can be scary
The fastest man in the world
Lived a happy life
And remained happily living
With his children and wife
Happiness is paramount
Fame can ruin people's lives.

He knew he was the fastest
And that knowledge he embraced.

When things are not going right in life, it can cause you to drink and smoke more than you may have otherwise. These words were inspired by this occurring.

I Don't Like What I Do

I don't like what I do like
I don't like what I do
Alcohol, smoking, my occupation too
Like it or not, I do!

I don't like what I do like
I don't like what I do,
It's all too much, but I cannot stop
It was enjoyed, but now destroys
And life it disrupts.

I want what I don't need
I want what I don't
If I don't get, won't lead to regret
No expectations need to be met.

I do, but then I don't
I will, but then I won't
I know I can, but then I can't
I like the chase but fear the chance.

I don't like what I do like
I don't like what I do
Alcohol, smoking, relationships too
Like it or not — it's true!

I get carried away — what can I say?
But I still do it.

I don't like what I did like
I don't like what I did
It was all too much, but I couldn't stop
Was enjoyed, but just destroyed
And life it disrupted.

'The Best' was written in contrast to 'The Fastest Man' mindset.

The Best

I'm in for the win
Can't stop when begin
Fired up, never quit
Hear the gun, start to run (*quick!*).

Non-stop, can't be beat
Hit the spot, I defeat
Negatives I neutralise
Wake-up and realise:

I am the best
"He's better than the rest"

Won't stop, fit as…
Focussed and I've got
The zest and desire
To beat the rest.

I won't fall, I won't turn back
On a roll — I own the track
I hit the spot, never slack
Give it all to have an impact.

I am the best!

Golden Anniversary

Wolves howl
Sheep bleat
Cows moo
But you
You, you just say nothing.

Kangaroos bounce
Horses trot
Frogs leap
But you…
You, you just sleep.

Crocodiles snap
Dogs bite
Cats scratch
But you…
You, you never react.

Clouds drift, clouds change shape
Clouds come and go
Clouds snow, clouds rain
But you…
You, you just stay the same.

The rain rains, time ticks by
We ask, "Why are we still together?"
Snow snows and whatever the weather
Who knows why?
Why do we stay together?

'Golden Anniversary' was written in 1990. It was written after seeing lots of unhappy old couples, married and still living together.

In contrast to 'Golden Anniversary' and 'Forever Together, Me And You', 'Beep! Beep!' is more of a light-hearted song about a new relationship that hasn't really developed into anything yet. I was trying to create music with a sports vibe, but the result was far from the mark. I disregarded the original task and conjured up this stranger kind of song.

Beep! Beep!

Hey there sweet
Do you wanna sit in my seat?
Wanna jump in my car?
While I drive you
Be my passenger
I wanna know how far you wanna go.

If you wanna take control
Grab hold of the wheel
If you wanna lead the way
Just put your foot down, let's go *hey!*

Not sure where
But we're going the same way
No rush, no fuss
Just feeling good today.
Don't wanna stop
Don't wanna hold back
We can go fast
We've been slow
Guess we've just gone with the flow.

Nothing now
In the way
But if there is
Gonna go beep! beep!

'Hot Dog' was originally called, 'Onion Man — Death By Quest For An Onion Lover', when written back in 1991. In 2022, when it was recorded as a song, the words were amended slightly, and additions made. This is when the title was also changed. It was inspired by adverts on TV, for food wanting to be eaten.

Hot Dog

See me, touch me, peel me, cry!
Fry me, taste me, eat me —
I'll die for you.

If you're hungry then I
Will fill you up, I'm your guy
If you're hungry, I'm your supper
Taste and please me hot dog lover.

See me, pick me — have a try
I'm your juicy hot dog guy
See me, pick me, have a taste
Don't let me go to waste.

See me — pick

me
You know you should
See me — taste me
You know I'm good.

Put the sausage in the gap
Squirt sauce on the baps
Then one more thing —
Time for the onion rings.

Saw me, touched me, feast begin
Cooked me up and let me in
Saw me, touched me, cooked me good
Between her lips I knew she would.

"Onion man, hot dog guy
Food for thought in her eye
Onion man - Frankfurter
She preferred to a burger."

She's the hot dog lover!
She's like no other
She's a hot dog lover and she wants another now —
Hot dog!

What is justifiable behaviour? And do all lives matter? And is there a God deciding our fate?

What Is Justice?

"All lives matter," said the serial killer
"Except the ones I killed.
Have you got a problem with that?
They got what they deserved."

Internet stalkers faking ID
Money scammers bleeding people dry
Bogus businesses that shouldn't exist
Cowboy companies taking the piss.

Money for work improperly done
Sickos on dating sites promising fun
Lives are ruined, lies are told
Money is conned out of innocent souls —
What is justice?

"Anarchy rules," said the anarchist
"And guns should be legal," so they shot him
"The police are racist," he screamed when arrested
After blowing-up a cop car — the black activist.
Freedom of speech is a civil right
"Religion is wrong" — Do you still agree with me?
Thank God I'm here, when so many have gone
Many good people, on Earth they belong,

But now in heaven, supposedly
But if they're in hell is that fair?
"All lives are equal" — are dead people equal too?

What is justice?

'You, explains and, even more so, justifies everything I did during the COVID period, while I had no job. This is about my fiancée, Debbie, who changed my life in so many ways and led to me writing lyrical poetry such as this. These are the lyrics that have the definitive line that answers the questions asked at the very beginning of this book.

You

I now know what (what)
Way to go, I've got (got)
What I lacked back (back)
Right on track…
Now, need no more
Unlike before
Got what I need
That's for sure.

What belongs is what exists
Got all I need, nothing is missed
Anymore, unlike before
She is everything and more.

What was needed to be done I did
To make life bearable throughout Covid
Got my act together and got things done
Made space for my new number one
That's you!

The one thing I needed
To feel I've succeeded
And continue to…
Is you.

'Forever Together, Me and You' was also written for my fiancée, who I must thank, for her major part in my life today and thus, making the whole of this book's concept complete.

Forever Together, Me and You

I never thought that I
Would meet somebody like you
That could pick me up
And make me feel brand new
Like you do.

I was feeling down
A bore to be around
But suddenly I changed
It's strange, but true
You brought me back to life
Something I thought no-one could do.

Sometimes, you know
The one for you
As soon as they show
And so, here we are
And here we go
Into the future
Forever together, me and you.

Each day is like a dream
So hard to believe
I'm the luckiest man alive
I never wanna die
Now you're in my life
I'll stay by your side.

You brought me back to life
I was close to death
My hopes had died
And nothing was left.

I knew
As soon as you
Sat next to me
The future was clear
And so, here we are
And here we go
Into the future
Forever together
Me and you.

'We Won't Stop' is the new version of 'Won't Stop!'. This includes an added section but, in this song, has a briefer chorus. This is known as 'The L And F Version' (The Lost And Found) due to the musical collaboration that created and played on this version of the song, in 2022. It was the only song on the album featuring another musician (on guitar and vocals). The original music I found on an old tape that Tim and I had used to record one of our jam sessions, back in the late 80s or 90s.

We Won't Stop!

Even when life is fading away
Our journey is here, in history
We just did our thing when the moments came
With no real intent, but fun was gained.

We hid in life but with a trace
Prints on the ribbon of brown were placed
Another era when raw was fresh
And rough was pure and fun was effortless.

It doesn't matter what they say
We'll continue to play.

We take breaks — long gaps of time
But behind the scenes we'll always find
Wherever we are, ideas will grow
But until we go
We know
We
Won't ever
Stop.

We won't stop!

Epilogue

This is my first book, consisting of lyrical poetry from all the songs on my 5 main albums, which were released between December 2019 and December 2022.

The second book will include every song featured on *'The Best of the Lost Connection 2011-2019, Parts 1 to 5', and 'The Lost And Found History (2021 Song Update)*. These 6 albums are compilations of unreleased songs (except 6 of the songs which were on '*Lost Property)*. These albums are not as conceptual as the ones in this book but do have a place in the bigger picture.

I also hope to release a book of poems, that were written as poems. This may include poems which I did actually turn into songs, though.